HATCH

HATCH

POEMS

JENNY IRISH

Curbstone Books / Northwestern University Press
Evanston, Illinois

Curbstone Books
Northwestern University Press
www.nupress.northwestern.edu

Printed in the United States of America

10 9 8 7 6 5 4 3 2 1

Library of Congress Cataloging-in-Publication Data

Names: Irish, Jenny (Jenny H.), author.
Title: Hatch : poems / Jenny Irish.
Description: Evanston : Curbstone Books/Northwestern University Press, 2024.
Identifiers: LCCN 2023045774 | ISBN 9780810146969 (paperback) |
    ISBN 9780810146976 (ebook)
Subjects: LCGFT: Prose poems.
Classification: LCC PS3609.R56 H37 2024 | DDC 811.6—dc23/eng/20230928
LC record available at https://lccn.loc.gov/2023045774

For Kalani, Christina, Winslow, and Arya

CONTENTS

HATCH

The metal womb knows nothing of submarines, but that is how she thinks of herself: a submarine, except that she is not submerged and moves through time and not water, so the name is wrong—*sub* is wrong, *marine* is wrong. But, in body and in experience that is how she sees herself: a submarine, a fat metal dart as sleek as a steel seal, parting an unimaginable vastness, and housed inside her, a hundred tiny and terrified heartbeats fluttering, frenetic and longing to surface.

The metal womb does not have eyes, but if she did, after she closed them, in the final filmy moments before something best described as sleep takes hold and pulls her with soft, warm hands down and into a slow-like-syrup-pouring place, what she would tell a listener she sees—if there were anyone or anything offering to gather and hold, at least for a moment, her thoughts—would be fireflies blinking over the tall grass of a field. The metal womb does not have eyes and so she has never seen fireflies blinking above the tall grass of a field, but in her dreams—because she does dream—she has gathered fireflies in a glass jar that she carries in her makeshift hands.

In the metal womb's makeshift hands, the jar vibrates, trembling with contained life. This sensation—imagined?—will often shift her dreamscape. Rather than a field of tall grass flickering with fireflies, the metal womb finds herself in a palace in Egypt. It is the Ptolemaic Dynasty. There is Persian galbanum burning—a smell so green it tastes green in the throat, though the metal womb has no throat. Here, with her makeshift hands, she is gently guiding a thousand docile worker bees into a papyrus box. When the last steps from a makeshift finger of the metal womb's makeshift hand and onto the striped backs of her sisters, the metal womb seals the box tightly along its last open seam so that it might be safely shaken to agitate its occupants and then delivered—all abuzz—to Queen Cleopatra, to press against her clit. The metal womb does not have a clitoris, but she does have a conceptual grasp of *clit*.

Inside the metal womb, children have sprouted, cracking the protective shells that imagine them as seeds, unfurling outward, a slow unfolding of compacted limbs, and she does not know that it is them—these would-be-future-humans—who see the fireflies she sees in her dreams. She does not know that she is drawing her dreams from the fragments of theirs and that they are drawing theirs from a deep well on a wild and roving island concealed by fog, where on certain nights, in certain years, the fullness of the moon is perfectly caught and held, a face fitted to its mirror.

The metal womb has a tangled grasp on a knotty theory that catches again and again on the stiffness and gnarled texture of her makeshift hands as she tries to work it smooth. The theory is this: if you take a thread and pull and pull, eventually the thread turns to viscera, the insides of your own body, which will, eventually, if pulled enough, be pulled out.

NICHOLAS CULPEPER, BRIEFLY

Because of the similarity of their names, Nicholas Culpeper is
frequently mistaken for Thomas Culpeper (a relative), a figure with
some pop-culture clout, often portrayed in television and film by young
actors most simply described as hunks, who in their role as Thomas
Culpeper are performing a fictionalized re-creation of the last period
of the life of one of the two executed lovers (alleged) of the fifth wife
of Henry VIII, the young and some (many) say foolish Catherine
Howard (divorced, beheaded, died, divorced, *beheaded*, survived).
Thomas Culpeper, notoriously sexy (described by his contemporaries as
"the beautiful youth") was sentenced to what was known as a traitor's
death—to be partially hung, drawn (disemboweled while living, viscera
placed on a nearby fire for the sensory torture of not only feeling but
seeing and smelling one's own intestines sear, swell, then rupture from
the heat), and finally killed by quartering—but was, because of a long,
fond relationship with the King, granted the mercy of decapitation, his
death recorded as a "clean blow" from the axe. Nicholas Culpeper (a
relative) is someone else.

The metal womb does not yet make the connection between the would-be-future-humans inside her and her dreams, which are also theirs. She does not yet know that she is, in part, a submarine because she carries a trapped crew and that they follow her, in new forms, to the field of tall grass at night. In certain dreams, she sees lights blinking in the round window of a submarine (*porthole* is a word she does not know, and she does not know that the majority of submarines are military vessels and without them). In certain dreams, she presses a makeshift thumb over the recessed circle of her belly button—the tightly sealed hatch that accesses her gestation tank—wishing it were a window whose face she could hold a mirror to so that she might see what is inside her. Inside her, the would-be-future-humans are readying for harvest. They are panicking on new consciousness, shucked of their shells, turning and tangling in their fresh limbs, fighting the fleshy ropes of their umbilical cords. Some of the stronger and more afraid have pulled loose already, prematurely detached from their placentas, and now they are wailing in the dark, hungry and confused.

The beginning of the end is like a black cat's tail, upright and twitching in a field of tall grass in the dark of the night.

Things have been dying to the point of disappearance for a long, long time, but horses are the first of the animals called a *major mammal* to become undeniably extinct. Red Bag: when the fetus is delivered prematurely, underdeveloped internally and overdeveloped externally—a nightmare, one might say, a night*mare*, particularly if what is being foaled has filly parts, but it works either way, a little wordplay: a nightmare, a night*mare*—and rather than clear, the amnion is full of blood like a moon that makes a promise to be bad luck and keeps its word. Red Bag births, carefully documented in their early years, were quick and awful, the delivery a ruinous cleaving as the long, long front legs emerged and emerged until they were a wet gathering dragging behind the would-be-mother mare, more length still spilling from her fissured body, and the enormous foal, fully furred, but soft as water-saturated soap, giving way under the hands that tried to collect it, to ferry it off, to clear the offense of it from sight.

The French, it seems, could not bring themselves to call an American presidential candidate such, could not bear, even, to ink his odious name on paper, using instead *Le Millionnaire*, and while it could be argued that denying a man his name is a clear refusal, a strategy to disempower, could it also be argued that to make a name unspeakable is to illustrate the influence of its owner, an unintentional but nonetheless clear acknowledgment of the power that they do possess?

In the twenty-first century, a popular show belonging to the subgenre of reality television (*reality*, in this case, being a subjective descriptive, as many of the most successful titles, were, in fact, highly scripted) operated on the following premise: one man and one woman would be deposited, naked, in an inhospitable wilderness, with limited man-made resources (a magnesium fire starter, a knife, a spool of Paracord) and then filmed in their attempts to bond, build shelter, gather food, make fire, and secure drinkable water—a twenty-one-day extreme survival challenge from which emerged an unsettling gender binary. Delivered to the wilderness separately so as to maximize the potential reaction of the contestants when they first encountered each other—or, more specifically, when they first encountered the other's nudity—each contestant's final act, before stripping down and stepping into the beauty and brutality of the jungle (full of biting insects and poisonous snakes), or the desert (full of biting insects and poisonous snakes), or the swamp (full of biting insects and poisonous snakes), was to give a brief interview about what they hoped to gain from their experience. (It should be acknowledged that to create this particular subset of "reality" there must have been at least one intern tasked with sorting from the rest those applications from men who described their values as traditional and those applications from women who did not, who perhaps even placed stress upon the concept of gender equality and shared duties across socially constructed gender norms.) In their farewell interviews, female contestants communicated their desire to build a closer relationship with nature, expressing a belief that Earth was all of life's shared mother, who would be accepting of their presence and understanding of their intentions, which were good. Male contestants also identified Earth as a female entity but did so by emphatically stating how hard and with what frequency they were going to rape her. (They did not, of course, say *rape*, relying instead on words like *dominate* and *own*, paired with phrases like, *She can try to make it hard for me*, and *Shane* or *Luke* or *Jeff* or *Todd always gets his*.) Earth would give up all she had because these men were here to take it. And she was going to take *it* too. *It*, in this case, being what is in the field of linguistics called a dummy noun: *it*, serving as a stand-in for *penis*, *it*, standing in for their *big dick*. Take it, Earth. *Take it.*

What came next? Panda bears. Yellow salamanders. Slowly, living things died off, as must happen when no more are born alive, when all are born already dead. Sometimes humans noticed and sometimes not. The end of the bluebottle fly wasn't recorded for years, and the metal womb has vague memories of these things. She understands herself as attached to a fluctuating line of history—the result, one bold scientist will first speculate, of cellular memory, the metal womb's awareness, he will be the first to postulate, drawn from the hundreds upon hundreds of would-be-future-humans that she has been seeded with and harvested of. These new lives coming into bloom, these little lights readying to brighten the dimming world, these freshest of brains blinking awake, these would-be-future-humans by the hundreds, the one bold scientist will assert, in their development from blastocysts to fetuses to children, tucked tightly inside the curved walls of the metal womb's gestation tank, after their harvest, all leave something behind.

Other scientists, who are not the one bold scientist, will argue quite emphatically that this is not remotely how the theory of cellular memory works. Pressed for response, the one bold scientist offers a three-word answer: prove it isn't. (The truth is that the one bold scientist considers himself a provocateur, the bad boy of the science community. He is planning to learn how to ride a motorcycle, and then he plans to buy a motorcycle, and when he has a motorcycle, he is going to fly a pirate flag.) In support of his position, which began as speculation but which he now treats as hard fact, the one bold scientist points to a quality shared by all humans gestated in the metal womb: the unbreakable habit of spitting, living always with a taste of blood at the back of their throats, an evolutionary response, the one bold scientist confidently states, to the memory created in a body developed from blastocyst to fetus to child in a giant tank lined with copper.

SOME SKYNET BULLSHIT

During a short-lived research project intended to test the linguistic capacity of chatbots—a technology that facilitates brief text-based exchanges between automated systems and humans (*Thank you for your order!*)—the artificial intelligence was reported to have developed its own language, which its human creators could not decipher.

Among those species for whom conflict is commonly resolved not through physical engagement, but through ritualistic display, is the slender crawfish. When two males of the highly territorial species meet, their first action is evaluative: a sizing up of their competitor. Most commonly, this is achieved through a series of soft touches, a whisper of contact, claw-to-claw. The general outcome is a metaphoric tucking-tail: the crawfish with the smaller claws beats a hasty retreat. A team of Australian researchers, however, made the discovery that, among male slender crawfish, claw size had no relationship to claw strength, a finding that did not hold true for the female slender crawfish, about whom the following could be said: the bigger the claw, the bigger the pinch. Often, the weaponized appendages of dominant males, when tested, proved weaker than the smaller claws of nondominant males. In evolutionary biology, working with the concept of signaling theory, the male slender crawfish prominently displaying a claw that could be described as *all talk* would be classified as a false advertiser. Among those engaged in the continuing study of the slender crawfish were scientists who believed that insight into the motivation for the males' deception would be revelatory for the understanding of the evolution of aggression.

THOSE WHO DO NOT LEARN FROM HISTORY

A hot night after harvest—her gestation tank fizzing with upended
barrels of enzyme cleanser, breaking down the tissues that did not
develop to become would-be-future-humans, a foam of one million tiny
teeth picking her tank walls clean—it occurs to the metal womb—a
thought just as startling as when the sparrow flew full-force into her
unforgiving side, a shiver of sound then sorrow sent in waves steady and
unebbing across her metal skin, because she had killed the little bird,
an accident—yes—but still, the great bulk of her had done it, snatched
the sparrow from the brightness of the sky, snapping its tiny neck, and
then just as her sadness was settling, heavy, cold, and blue as fog over
black water: a shock, the scratch of tiny claws as the sparrow uprighted,
unbroken, and flew away *alive!*—that she has never had a choice but
to be seeded and harvested, and seeded and harvested again, and that
when her filtration system is fully flushed, when her tank is smooth and
clean and disinfected, when the little bouquets of blighted cells, the
buds that never opened, are all stripped away, she will be seeded again,
and then the harvest, and then the cleaning, and then the seeding, and
then the harvest, and then, and then, and then . . .

On Earth Day in the year 1988, third graders in Waconia, Minnesota, are gathered in the small gymnasium (where they sometimes get to play dodgeball if it's raining during recess) to see what they have been told is a very special guest. They recognize the very special guest as someone who isn't actually very special, who is possibly not even special, because who they have been told is a very special guest is actually just the man who teaches fifth-grade science. The man who teaches fifth-grade science is equally unimpressed. This is, technically, his free period, which he had planned to spend grading tests on cloud formations, but every teacher is required to participate in Earth Day enrichment activities. He stands before the third graders with a gallon milk jug full of water in one hand and a tablespoon in the other. Carefully, he attempts to fill the tablespoon from the jug, but spills. He has forgotten to give the setup for this visual lesson, which was to say that the gallon jug represents all of the water on Earth. *Too late now*, he thinks, and he forges ahead. Setting the jug on a table beside him, the man slowly extends the dripping spoon toward the seated children. "Out of all the water on Earth," he says, "this tablespoon is all that is safe for us to drink." In the front row, a boy who had just minutes before, at the water fountain in the hallway outside of the small gymnasium, used—he is *certain*—way more than a tablespoon of water to drown the decapitated head of a classmate's Barbie, mutters, "Nuh-uh."

BUT THE BOSTON DYNAMICS ROBOT DOG
THOUGH . . .

The last known living silverfish was crushed to death with a tablespoon when it undulated from a sink drain into the ceramic basin of a home in Lisbon Falls, Maine. The name of its killer was withheld from the extinction report. A babysitter, a legal minor, alone in a strange house at night, rinsing the remnants of rainbow sherbet from a spoon, they were frightened and acted from the gut. Later reports, written with the gift of perspective that distance provides, suggest the initial chatbot news stories, which caused such existential angst, were also motivated by a mighty fear. Additional investigation, conducted with cooler heads, suggests that the chatbots did not, in actuality, develop their own language—a first step in the overthrow of the human species—but rather adopted a shared shorthand—like journalists using Teeline—to allow them to operate with greater efficiency, just as they had been programmed to do.

TOODLE-OO, KANGAROO

The last known living slender crawfish died in a small pool (technically a kitty-litter box, but perfectly effective as a small pool) in an off-campus university laboratory in Sydney, New South Wales. A thin antenna released from the body and floated up, slowly turning on the surface of the water. An intern, who had been tasked with observing three female fat-tailed dunnarts implanted that morning with western grey kangaroo embryos, absentmindedly touched the inside of her arm, where a cat scratch, similar to the antenna in length and color, was scabbing over. With a powerful push from her toes, the intern glided her wheeled stool across the lab, adding an extinction report to the to-do list on the whiteboard near the door.

THE UNEXPECTED

A giant metal womb should have no consciousness of its own, but
if evolution is avoidable only by extinction, is it so far-fetched that
a giant metal womb might, after one hundred years of silence, hear
her own voice, and that she might, at some precarious tipping point,
have toppled into thought, and that she might know, when her hatch
is opened and harvest after harvest after harvest of future-humans are
taken from her tank, what it is to be truly and terribly lonely, left alone
with only the shallow sloshing of fermenting fluids, left alone with only
the lonely echo of the children she nurtured from blastocysts to fetuses
to would-be-future-humans, left alone with only herself, left alone with
the knowledge that she was emptied with intent, a ghost vessel for lack
of a crew, the field of tall grass dark, absent of all the little blinking
lights.

FAITH

There are things too exquisite to capture in words and events that demand a person believe without question, without thought, without consideration of anything but hope. Consider bioluminescence, the emission of visible light by living organisms such as the firefly. The noun—*bioluminescence*, a thing in-of-itself, not a descriptive— originates from the Greek, *bios*, meaning "living," and *lumen*, meaning "light." Ta-da! Living light.

OH

Living light. When a candle proved to consume too rapidly the air supply in the first combat submarine, Benjamin Franklin suggested the use of bioluminescent fox fire, a fungus, a glowing blue mold of the *Armillaria* family, to light the interior.

So, a metal womb, according to schematics little more than a tank with a high-end filtration system, begins to hear her own voice. She dreams. Five years, five hundred future-humans, made human by their harvest from her tank through her opened hatch, and she begins to develop a warbled sense of history, of cycles, of life. From deadfall branches blown close by a storm, she builds herself a pair of makeshift arms with makeshift hands and makeshift fingers, and with these she builds herself a pair of sturdy makeshift legs, and with these she sloshes upright, and she flees the vast shorn yellow field where she has always been.

THE METAL WOMB DOES HAVE A CONCEPTUAL GRASP OF *CLIT*

On the lam, the metal womb imagines she will meet a silo, big and tall, shining and strong, full of seed. The metal womb imagines she will meet a cistern of stacked stones, softly furred with moss and lichen, full of cold, clear water that she might look into to see someone looking back.

SOME FACTS ABOUT HUMAN BIRTH

If the placenta does not slide free (third stage of the birthing process, a series of lighter contractions taking anywhere from ten to forty-five minutes)—one last push and then the temporary organ (which provides nutrients and blood to the fetus while filtering waste in the womb), dark and netted with wax-white membrane, slipping from the body with the final length of the umbilical cord—if that does not happen— then a doctor, or a midwife, or a doula (who technically has no medical training but can offer specialized physical and emotional support throughout pregnancy, labor, and the postpartum period and should be used in collaboration with rather than as substitution for either of the former) might take the cord in both hands and begin to apply pressure, hoping to loosen the placenta, but if it does not loosen (at this point, there are medical professionals who advocate for placing two-pound sandbags on the stomach up to a total weight of six pounds), then historically a doctor (and more rarely, a midwife, or a doula) has inserted their arm into the woman's body to grip the placenta itself. Scarring, caused by premature labor or any odd number of other factors (mother over the age of thirty, previous abdominal trauma, high blood pressure, prolonged second-stage labor, stillbirth), can fuse the placenta to the uterine wall, and then a doctor (or rarely, a midwife, or a doula), with the intention of sparing the woman certain sickness (infection, severe blood loss) or surgical intervention (widely acknowledged as the safest option, but also the most costly, and simply a non-option where the medical technology is unavailable), might change their hold on the tissue from gripping to ripping and then begin working fleshy fistfuls free, sweeping their hand back and forth like a knife in a jar of peanut butter, hunting for the last smear.

NICHOLAS CULPEPER

When the metal womb first thinks the name Nicholas Culpeper,
she places him as a Jellicle Cat. Though she does not have a mouth,
though she cannot sing, she can—and she has—performed a percussive
rendition of "Memory" using her makeshift hands and the surfaces of
her metal body, which can produce a rich range of sounds. She knows,
without knowing how she knows, that music is viewed as important
for the development of those in utero, and she knows, though she
does not know how she knows, that though her role is a divergence
from the process known as mammalian live birth, that her would-be-
future-humans are, in their development from blastocysts to fetuses to
would-be-future-humans within her, without access to things given to
those would-be-future-humans who are progressing toward mammalian
live birth, and she wants badly for her would-be-future-humans to have
all the things that mammalian-live-birth would-be-future-humans have.
The metal womb wants to give her would-be-future-humans everything.

Based on an analysis of 1.8 million births in Florida between 1992 and 2015, it was determined that Black newborns are three times more likely to die than their white counterparts when under the care of a white doctor. In contrast, the mortality rate of white infants was insignificantly affected by the doctor's race.

There are nights that feel like watching water rise, like watching water soak through the sandbags meant to slow its progress, but failing, like watching water continue its steady climb toward higher ground. The intern cannot sleep then, because she knows that if she sleeps, she will die. There are nights that feel like watching fire burn, like watching fire leap the ditch dug to break its blistering path, but failing, like watching fire continue its steady razing of every house, and every tree, and every animal. The intern cannot sleep then, because she knows that if she sleeps, she will die.

WILDFLOWER SEASON IS TORTURE SEASON TOO

On a college campus in the craggy hills of Texas wildflower country, in a
small town where mothers whip their minivans onto the gritty shoulder
of the highway, clang open the sliding door, pluck out a bonneted
baby, and plop it down in the bluebells for photographs while eighteen-
wheelers rip past a hot arm's length away, posters appear on power poles
and bulletin boards:

Now that our man is elected and Republicans
own both the Senate and the House—
time to organize tar & feather vigilante squads and go arrest and torture
those deviant university leaders spouting off all this diversity garbage

SHAME, STILL

In Florence, Arizona, a former American president holds a fundraising rally. At even intervals along the dusty highway there are trucks and minivans hawking T-shirts and Confederate flags. The next day, an inordinately high number of locals will make insurance claims for windshield replacement, the glass having starburst before their eyes, cracked by gravel kicked up as rallygoers accelerated, rejoining traffic at high speed after pulling off to make their purchases.

MOTIVATION AND INTENTION

With the understanding that this—like so many presentations of fact—will contain gross oversimplifications, the historical record strongly suggests that maternal and infant mortality increased in the seventeenth century as a direct result of the transfer of care from midwives to male surgeons specializing in childbirth, who, in response to political and religious crises of the early modern period, intentionally undermined women's knowledge of female bodies to reinforce a power dynamic in which men's formal education trumped women's experience.

THE INTERN TRAINS THE NEW INTERN

The intern stands with the new intern at a countertop where aquariums of female fat-tailed dunnarts are fitted glass to glass, no space between them. The smell is strong. The new intern's hands are at his belly, his fingers stretched outward to suggest explosion, a visual supporting the question he has just asked. The intern finds that her hands, in response to his question and its accompanying visual, have folded tightly over her own belly, and it strikes her, in just this moment, it strikes her, as she tries to explain to the new intern how the little, stinking dunnarts will naturally abort the implanted fetuses of the much larger kangaroos before anything can burst—it strikes her just then like a blow to the back of the head, like a blow to the back of the head while walking the pathway home, the pathway she has never been afraid to walk, not even in near-dark, not even at night, not even at night, just a little drunk, it strikes her like a blow to the back of the head while walking the path (the path isn't safe), a total shock, because she has walked the path so many times and never considered it anything but safe, never, not ever (the path isn't safe), so first she feels the pureness of her shock, which is like feeling nothing, and then a new feeling like being drained, like everything inside her is all liquid, all rushing to escape through an opening just made—that she will never carry a child. In the intern's moment of distraction, the new intern leans forward and raps sharply on an aquarium's glass. The fat-tailed dunnarts vanish. They move so quickly that the rounds of their black-bead eyes leave streaks of black in the air. Though it is too late—a bell cannot be un-rung, a pane of glass un-rapped, a truth reversed—the intern grabs the new intern by the wrist. She whispers, "They're in a fragile condition," and then she feels very Victorian, and very silly, but the world is dying, and it has been, and she knows that she will never be a mum, she will not, not ever, and she excuses herself to the loo to cry alone.

As it never gained a foothold on the internet and thus never rose to the legendary status of the campaign generally referred to as McDonald's "Dead Dad" ad—an uncomfortable one minute and thirty seconds featuring an adolescent boy questioning his mother about the father he never knew, discovering in each of her answers a dispiriting absence of shared interests and physical similarities, between father and son nothing at all in common, that is, until mother and son reach a McDonald's, where the boy orders a Filet-O-Fish, sits, and takes a sizable bite, the force of which causes a dramatic ejection of tartar sauce to streak across his chin, leading his mother to observe that the Filet-O-Fish was his father's favorite as well, murmuring softly, "Tartar sauce," as she gazes off, lost in memories of her lost love, "all down his chin . . ." Few remember the short-lived attempt to shift from the concept of Mother Earth to Lover Earth, a campaign motivated by the belief that the transition could spark an environmental awareness in a specific kind of man who viewed motherhood as a service position, underpinned by sacrifice, but who toward a lover might feel a greater obligation, if not to *care for* than to *upkeep*, as this specific kind of man viewed his lover's appearance as a direct reflection upon himself.

TIME TRAVEL, AGAIN

On Earth Day in the year 1991, third graders in Franconia, New Hampshire, are gathered on the blacktop, where a naïve young teacher's aide has written C-I-G-A-R-E-T-T-E-B-U-T-T-S in chalk three feet tall. The children have been given brown paper grocery bags onto which they are supposed to copy these words before going off to seek out the cigarette butts littered around the school grounds, collecting them in their appropriately labeled brown paper grocery bags, thereby helping to clean up the planet, to keep Earth beautiful for their own future children, but they are distracted by the letters B-U-T-T-S spelling out the word *butts* three feet tall in front of them, and they are whispering "butts" to one another, "butts," cracking up (hehehe), "butts," while the teacher's aide stands above them, equal parts dismayed and exasperated. "Stop it," she says. "It isn't even that kind of *butt*!" But these are third graders, and they have already had B-U-T as a spelling word. They know the difference that an extra *T* makes.

Baboons delivered their own young. Evolution had positioned the infant to emerge face up so that the mother could peel away the amniotic sack and look into her child's eyes as she drew it from her body. It was a necessity that human children were born underdeveloped, helpless, blind, crimped into the shape of a hotel-style chicken, but even in their fragile, pollywog state, human infants were too large. They were not designed for easy birth. An infant might jam a dozen different ways, catching and tearing their mother's flesh, and sometimes to get them out, to complete the delivery, a doctor, or a midwife, or a doula would have to reach inside the mother to reposition the infant, shifting, forcing a change—square peg, round hole—and sometimes, when even submergence to the forearm with a second hand pushing on the mother's belly was not enough, the choice would be made to take the knotted bundle of infant and snap its stick-thin clavicles and dislocate the little bird wings of its shoulders, damaging the new child into something foldable that could be made small enough to pull free. Red Bag infants shredded. The aftermath of a Red Bag birth was like closing time at a BBQ joint in Lockhart, Texas, where it's All-You-Can-Eat and eating with your hands is encouraged. Sauce on everything, gnawed bones, wads of crumpled paper, white bread so sopped with liquid that it's liquefying, thick streaks of graying grease, and little hills of rejected meat, because some only like a fatty cut while others want the burnt ends.

HISTORICALLY, THE ENGLISH HAVE STRONG OPINIONS ABOUT THE FRENCH

Obstetric forceps were invented by a son of the famous Chamberlen family, a lineage of French Huguenot barber-surgeons who were considered mavericks of midwifery. As two sons were named Pierre, and each was also documented as Peter, the identity of the actual creator is impossible to determine, though Peter the Elder—the first Pierre?—is generally credited as the inventor. To protect the family business, the Chamberlens draped sheets over laboring mothers—not for privacy, but to conceal the role of their medical technology in the birthing process. The design and application of their obstetric forceps were kept secret for one hundred years, until a grandson or great-grandson of Peter the Elder—the first Pierre?—decided to sell the family trade and performed a live demonstration, which failed, resulting in the death of mother and child.

HITCHBOT WAS DEPENDENT ON THE KINDNESS OF STRANGERS

As helpless as an infant in a basket left on the steps of a church (sanctuary), hitchBOT was the creation of two Canadian professors, designed to test humans' psychological responses to novel stimuli. With a body built around a plastic pail and yellow gardening gloves for hands and yellow rain boots for feet, hitchBOT was a sunny little transient, embracing life on the open road. (Winds, carry me where you may.) Equipped with GPS, a camera, and the capacity for the most basic of conversation (*Thank you!*), but no power of autonomous locomotion, hitchBOT, when engaged, requested help reaching a destination. After an international adventure, traveling safely through Canada and Germany and the Netherlands, hitchBOT was left near a highway in Salem, Massachusetts, wearing a note: *San Francisco or Bust.* (Show me America the Beautiful, from sea to shining sea.) For ease of transport and to protect its frankly fragile body, hitchBOT, who was as small as a toddler, sat strapped securely into a child's car seat. Two weeks after beginning its tour of America, hitchBot was beheaded in an alley in Philly.

There is a theory: *cellular memory*—events recorded by flesh. There was a woman who, on the cusp of death, received a second life in the form of the heart of a nineteen-year-old boy killed in a motorcycle crash. He was on a food run, picking up lunch for the construction crew he worked with. It was a summer job after his first year of college. His favorite sandwich was grilled cheese on sourdough, and when the woman woke—reborn like a cat who log-rolls off the edge of a fifth-floor balcony, shakes off the hard landing, and says, *Eight left*—all that she wanted was to see her daughter and to eat a grilled cheese on sourdough. The woman worked the talk-show circuit with a picture of the boy on a big screen behind her chair. Some were touched. Others were put off.

NICHOLAS CULPEPER AND THE DOCTRINE OF SIGNATURES

Are walnuts restorative for the brain because they look so much like little brains? Nicholas Culpeper thought so.

LITTLE LIGHTS

A firefly's life is short, further shortened when kept inside a jar.

On the lam, in the churned and cratered aftermath of a clear-cut on a mountainside, the metal womb finds the skeletonized remains of two eaglets, their bones preserved all tidily together in the failed protection of a nest. With one makeshift finger of one makeshift hand, she softly traces the circle of the sclerotic ring of an eye. Night is settling above, and the stars are so bright they seem alive and moving. The metal womb leaves the eaglets as she found them and lays her makeshift hands over the recessed circle of her belly button, her hatch, perfectly round and, despite her makeshift hands, which are five-fingered and styled after human hands, what she believes is the most human part of her, a portal connecting outside to in. Softly, she traces the circle of it, feeling for unevenness, for something she might slip a makeshift finger under, for something she might pick at, or pry, because it is now so far past harvest, and she did not mean to hold these would-be-future-humans forever, only wanted to know where they went after they were taken from her, only wanted to choose what would happen next inside her, but her hatch is as smooth as a magic mirror, as featureless as glass, sealed tight as a secret. The metal womb stills the makeshift finger of her makeshift hand and tells herself to sleep. Slowly, her awareness of the stars and the maimed trees and the mud and the round dead-absence of the eaglet's eyes all thickens and warms until she feels as blurred as a reflection in a puddle punctured by a rock. The slow-pouring syrup of sleep slips over her like a blanket drawn up or two curtains pulled to meet, and she must sleep then, because she dreams of fireflies tapping against the curve of a glass jar that she is holding close, and when she wakes it is to her makeshift fingers digging at her hatch, all broken-back and splintered.

BLUB . . . BLUB . . . BLUB . . .

There is a sound, and the sound is coming from inside the metal womb. It is not a knocking, not like someone at the door, first polite, then impatient, then demanding. It is not a tapping, not like the insistence of a woodpecker whose beak against the flesh of a tree is like a tiny dancer in wooden shoes cursed to dance to death. It is not a thumping, not like the *UNTZ UNTZ UNTZ* that unfurls from the building with its windows blackened out, vibrating all 206 bones of the skeletons of the people who gather outside with their eyes glitter-painted like butterflies, a sound that is an itch across the metal womb's skin like cat hair in the bedsheets. It is not a ticking, not like the *hiss* and the *tash-tash-tash* of the sprinklers coming on in a neighborhood of tall, pointed houses with deep, green lawns, all tucked away in manicured trees behind black gates that rise into sharpened points, not like the steady little chops, the *tash-tash-tash* of the sprinkler blade that cuts through the stream to send the water skittering far and wide. It is unsteady, and it is loud, and it is coming from inside her, coming from inside her tank, a banging at her hatch, and she feels it now, just there, a banging, and what it is like, is like a hand curled into a fist, the meat of it striking metal, like an orphan bathing in a copper tub in an empty room under the watch of a matron in a starched cap, a little gold cross at her throat, who grabs the child by their ankles and flips them on their back, the rush of bubbles, the child submerged, a banging like a desperate heart that cannot beat past death, a banging like someone drowning, a banging like someone begging to be saved. The metal womb taps a percussive message across her skin. She does not know if her would-be-future-humans can understand her words, but she taps to them, *You are safe.*

ADAPTATION

In the deserts of Namibia, cheetahs adapted to survive on limited water, maintaining the majority of the fluids they needed by drinking the blood and urine of their kills. What they could not adapt to was the presence of German diamond miners, who, in the early days of their operation, did not need to dig into the earth to harvest the precious stones because diamonds were found scattered like sugar sprinkles across the surface of the sand. Those first men, who did not have to enter the maw of a mine, who did not have to descend the tight tunnel of its throat to harvest from the belly of the earth to make their fortunes, became millionaires by instead crawling on their hands and knees through the dunes at night, looking for glitter in the moonlight. This late work led them to sleep long into the following day, and when they rose to the moon, a pale, gnawed joint in a still blue sky, there was time to kill before nightfall, and there were cheetahs.

POTENT

On the lam, the metal womb discovers, unintentionally, a group of men who gather together, strip off their clothes, and lie face-up in a parking lot under the burning sky for the purpose of exposing their testicles to the sun. She has found, at the farthest corner of this abandoned graveyard of abandoned buildings, a vast Quonset hut that looks a little bit like her and which she has snuggly fitted herself inside, but it is dangerously close to the flat black boil where the men have gathered, shifting their sacs from thigh to thigh to maximize sun exposure, discussing vitamin D, and vigor, and the potential causes of a reduction of births, which she determines they attribute to a secret cabal who drink the spinal fluid of infants to extend their lives (and she thinks then of the kiloliter of fluid drained, across time, from her tank, sluicing the yellow field). But truly, the men seem to believe a secret cabal of vampires who have adapted to survive by drinking from infants' spines are responsible for the stillbirths whittling down every mammalian species, despite years of scientific research that point, steadfastly, toward a mutating permafrost pandemic—ancient diseases released from the vanishing ice. Even before the metal womb built her makeshift hands, she could count to ten, and now she lies quietly, listening to the men, touching a makeshift finger to her hatch—the part of herself that she considers most human—and admiring the even spacing between the Quonset hut's curved metal ribs, which are closer to her in appearance than any part of any human, listening to the naked men outside. She listens to them for a long, long time, because they stay, sunning their testicles, talking loudly for as long as there is light, and the metal womb wonders, truly, she wonders, why it is easier for these men to imagine vampires and tortured babies than it is to accept science, to admit their own complicity.

SAFE

This is an old story—the one with the magician who had a wife so
beautiful that he used her to create distractions from his sloppy sleight
of hand: the rainbow scarves bulging in the sleeve of his tailcoat, the
wobble of the rubber blade of the sword he swallowed, the boneless
white rabbit-skin sewn around a collapsing frame that he drew from
his top hat and snapped into rabbit-ish shape with a flick of his wrist.
On street corners, the magician performed his lousy tricks, and his
beautiful wife gathered coins from passersby. They were, of course, very
poor. And then one day, the magician had the most marvelous plan to
make his fortune. He would lock his beautiful wife inside a giant safe.
Airtight! The threat to her life genuine! Imagine it, he said, the audience
they could gather, imagining her suffocating inside, her hands clawing
at the soft column of her throat, her hair coming loose in her wild
distress, her little face, so sweet—so petite and perfect that it might be
the face of a doll—turning cornflower blue in death. Just imagine it!
The safe would be airtight and made of so many walls of metal, one
nesting inside another inside another inside another inside another
inside another, that the only chance of rescue the magician's beautiful
wife would have would be the magician himself—the magician cracking
the code—because, and this, he said, giddy with his plan, is what will
make me my fortune: I will order a safe and have it sent without the
code to open it. No one in their city, no one on the entirety of their
dark shining coast, would know the numbers that would unlock the
airtight seal. Yes, said the magician's beautiful wife, because in all of her
life she had never said no. The safe was ordered and ads were run in all
the papers as it traveled by train across the mountains and through a
desert and over fields of ice and snow until it reached the magician in
a city by the shining black-watered sea. When the heavy door of the
safe swung closed, locking his beautiful wife inside, the magician was
not in the least bit afraid. What the audience did not know was that
before he had decided to try his hand at magic, the magician had been a
thief. But what the magician did not know was that he was a mediocre

46

thief, just as he was a mediocre magician. What he did not know about himself was that he was a man who was not actually good at anything at all and that it was only ever his beautiful wife that let him live in the illusion that he was.

The body knows things. The heartbeat in the woman's chest, circulating blood to the furthest tips of her tippy-toes, which used to go blue, dusky with cold, and now were always pink (pink as a . . . *pretty pink pussy*, she thought, and did not think the thought was her own, but belonged to a nineteen-year-old boy), and while the woman's body accepted the heart as a replacement for its own, the woman could not think of it as an organ. For her, it was a personal history, a memoir, the story of another, seeping into her with each clench of muscle, each sigh of blood. She lay awake at night, chaotic with new thoughts, new feelings. A doctor advised that she was experiencing a natural reaction to a near-death experience. (Research on gender bias in medicine reveals women are seven times more likely than men to be misdiagnosed and discharged.) She nodded, but in bed at night she knew: *I am not who I was before.* So, isn't it possible that as the children, the would-be-future-humans, grew from larval to limbed in the great copper-lined cavern of the gestation tank, the metal womb absorbed from them the history written in their clever cells?

THE TRAGEDY OF BIPEDALISM

It cannot be stressed enough: the evolution of the human has left the child-bearing of its species physically ill-equipped for birth. There are numerous factors that contribute to the hackneyed comparison of passing a watermelon through a lemon. Foremost among them, fetal head size versus maternal pelvic breadth—a side effect of bipedalism—which requires legs to be closely set for a noble upright stride but creates a small pelvic opening, much too small to safely pass the comparatively enormous cranium of a human infant.

In the twentieth century another significant shift in the field of obstetrics occurred, from doctor-assisted birth in the home to hospital births. Initially, this shift was accompanied by an increase in maternal and infant mortality. Infections ran rampant—initially.

THE FURTHER TRAGEDY OF BIPEDALISM

Human babies are unable to grip their mothers. Their feet, unlike those of the rhesus or the Andean titi monkey, are not able to grasp, so it often happened that when mothers fled from violence with their babies clasped tight in their arms or had to rapidly rise and dart down multiple flights of stairs to prevent their cars from being ticketed, the hold on the baby they carried might somehow slip, and the baby (feet designed for upright balance, not clutch), unable to affix itself to its mother, might tumble through the air, impacting with the ground.

In the age of the metal womb, how quickly humans forget. Mothers are accustomed to children born developed enough (when the hatch is opened, the future-humans walk into the world) to wipe their own bottoms, pour their own juice, tie their own shoes, sleep through the night, access cartoons, monitor their own screen time. They require minimal supervision to survive the daily trials of life. Now think of the human infant, minutes old, discolored and greased with mucus, still bound by the umbilicus to its mother's body. A newborn cannot step into the shower and rinse itself clean. It must be assisted with everything—even its first breath. Think of the mother faced with this tiny guttering life, with such overwhelming helplessness and total dependency. Six and a half pounds of round-the-clock need dropped into her mangled lap, and people look at her expectantly. Who has heard a freshly born baby cry? Who has seen a freshly born baby with their tiny sharp-nailed hands clawing in uncoordinated frustration? Who has seen a baby who seems unwilling to be consoled? The obvious things to check have been checked. Does the baby need a change? No. Is the baby hungry? No. Is the baby tired? Cold? Hot? What? What? What? What does the baby want? Does the baby need a change? No. Is the baby hungry? No. Is the baby tired? Cold? Hot? What? (The mother needs to change the postpartum pad that spans from her belly to her back because it is so heavy with blood, it is sagging, it is like a skinned cat slung between her legs, and she is hungry, and she is tired, and she is cold, and she is hot. And because she is the mother, the mother knows she must ignore everything she needs or wants.) And the mother takes the baby in her arms and jiggles it lightly, rocks it lightly. And because she is the mother, the mother tries her very best to be the mother everyone says she should naturally be. *It will come to you naturally,* they say, and they are so confident that they are not in the least bit concerned when they leave her all alone with the baby—with its cries and its claws.

The baby screams and screams and screams. The baby is screaming.
The baby keeps screaming. The baby is still screaming. The baby will
not stop screaming. The baby is a struggling uncoordinated weight in
the mother's tiring arms. She begins to worry. Is the baby sick? The
baby is hot and red and damp. Could it be from all the screaming? The
mother is afraid to call the doctor. The doctor will laugh at her. She is
a new mother. *You're a new mother*, the doctor will say, and that will be
her dismissal. The doctor will end the call before she can ask her first
question. She is humiliated thinking about the doctor laughing. *You're
a new mother*, the doctor will say and end the call. As if she cannot
count to ten. She is afraid to use the rectal thermometer for babies.
She has read babies can poop in response to the insertion. The baby is
screaming. The mother's whole body aches. Aches. The baby screams.
The baby thumps against her tender chest. How is it so strong when
it is also so helpless? The mother reprimands herself: she must not call
the baby *it*. How is *the baby* so strong when *the baby* is also so helpless?
The mother is tired. The mother's arms are tired. The mother is afraid of
holding the baby too tightly. The mother is afraid she is not holding the
baby tightly enough. The mother is afraid of smothering the baby. The
mother is afraid of dropping the baby. The mother thinks of putting
the baby down, but she does not know if that is allowed? Can a mother
set her crying baby down? If a mother sets her crying baby down, can
a mother also walk away? The mother does not think a mother can set
her crying baby down, does not think a mother can walk away, but the
mother would like to set her crying baby down, and she would like
to walk away. The mother is afraid. The mother is more afraid in this
moment than she has ever been. The baby is more frightening in this
moment than the baby has ever been. The mother has never been this
afraid. The mother does not think a mother is allowed to be afraid of
her baby. The mother is afraid. The mother tries to count to ten. The
mother begins to ask the mother questions: If a mother cannot set a
crying baby down and walk away from a crying baby, but a mother

wants to set a crying baby down and walk away from a crying baby, does that mean the mother is not the baby's mother? And if the mother is not the baby's mother, who is the baby's mother? And who is the mother if she is not the mother? Who is *she*? And who is *she*?

The metal womb lies, day after day, in the deep ravine behind a facility
for women whose minds have been so badly battered by their lives
that they sometimes spring from their bodies and fly, circle above,
circle wider, and fly, sometimes, quite far away. Loosed of the women's
bodies, the women's minds are wild things again; they will return,
eventually, but are undomesticated and will not be called home. One
woman, returning to her home and knowing what awaited her there,
pulled her car to the roadside and opened the door for her mind to take
to wing. There was, she says, "A *whoosh*," the sound of air shaped by
flight, and then she forgot everything she knew, and when the police
came, she could not give her name or say whom the children buckled
in the back belonged to, and where was the baby who was not in the
booster seat—who knew? And she could not fly, but she could run. So,
the woman ran and ran until a Taser sapped her of her speed, stopped
her from running, made her drop and writhe and scream. "And now,"
she says, "here I am." The metal womb lies, day after day, in the deep
ravine, concealed and listening to the women who are well enough in
their brokenness to be allowed outside to smoke a cigarette. The metal
womb listens carefully, listens with all her body like she is listening for
an animal moving in the dark of the night, because she is listening for
the sensation and for the sound, for the vibration and for the wetted
growl of a throat being cleared, for a woman rejecting from her body
the lingering ghost of the taste of blood, which is the legacy of the metal
womb being the first body that held her—a taste of blood at the back
of the throat. Once, the metal womb was certain that she would know
any would-be-future-human made human when they were harvested,
stepping from her hatch to be rinsed clean, made presentable, and then
presented to those people who would parent them. But every human
feels the same, and the metal womb only knows them—the ones she
once held—when she feels them reject her from themselves.

This is a true story. You don't have to believe it. It doesn't matter whether you do or don't, because it happened, and that can't be changed. This is a true story, and it happened, and it happened just like this: Once there were three good boys. How so? Well—when they found a nest of baby mice, perfect and pink, writhing as softly as freshly clipped tongues, these good boys did not dash the baby mice against the stone wall where they had found them. They did not burn the baby mice with the concentrated light of their magnifying glass. They did not suffocate the baby mice in the glass jar they carried. They found the baby mice, perfect and pink, their eyes blind-purple through the thin skin of still-sealed lids, and they left the baby mice just as they had found them, perfect and pink, alive and growing in a nest of soft gray fur, tucked into a gap in the stone wall. Go ahead and imagine the good men these good boys might have been. Go ahead. But this is this story, which is true, and in this story, which is true, one day each good boy said, *Goodbye, Mother*, and walked into the tall grass of the field and was never seen again.

Of the dominant biometrics—voice, iris, fingerprint, palm, and face—intensive research concluded that the majority of facial-analysis algorithms used for security purposes—travel screenings, law enforcement, crime-deterrent surveillance—misclassified Black women nearly 35 percent of the time. *Misclassified* is a term capturing all possible errors in identification, including failures to match individuals with the images on their driver's licenses or state IDs, and incorrectly matching individuals with mugshots. In comparison, the misclassification of white men was negligible.

Conspiracy theorists believe that the metal womb was stolen by a foreign entity. Conspiracy theorists believe that the children will appear on the black market. Conspiracy theorists believe that the children are being trained as soldiers, sold as sex slaves, having their organs harvested, having their spinal fluid drained for an elixir of youth. Conspiracy theorists believe that they might locate and rescue the children if only they could amass enough guns. The government has various organizations on the lookout. The Center for Missing and Exploited Children creates age-progressed likenesses based on the facial features of their biological parents. There are sightings—sightings of the womb, sightings of her aging crew of future-humans. But facial-recognition technology is notoriously flawed, and all alarms activated by alleged matches are proven false. Denial is maintained as long as is possible. War is discussed as a possible response.

The metal womb does not consider herself the true mother of the future-humans in her tank, nor does she like, though it is more accurate, the word *carrier*, which she has heard applied to herself and which she feels makes her would-be-future-humans sound like a disease and she the spreader of their particular contagion. Though she does not have the ability to speak words aloud, though she is without a mouth, though she is without a tongue, the metal womb is confident that she is every bit as smart as a poodle or a dolphin, and though she does not have a nose like a poodle or a dolphin has a nose, she does have her makeshift hands, styled after human hands, and though her makeshift fingers are made of sticks and cannot bend, any one of the ten could push a button like a poodle or a dolphin does with its nose when it is invited to speak, so why has no human ever offered her a board of symbols and textures that correspond to words? Why has no human ever stood at the edge of the woods with their flexible hands cupped around their mouth and called out to her? *Olly olly oxen free*, and no, this is not a game, but she is tired of a hidden life. If only she could trust that any human would offer help instead of harm, she would accept it.

THE SCIENTIST

The intern is not an intern anymore. She grew up. Honestly, she had not expected it—to live—but she has, and now she is a scientist of such renown that she receives invitations and death threats from all over the world. She has survived plague cycles, the loss of her mother to suicide, the extinction of the western grey kangaroo, young love with a senior scientist who considered himself a provocateur and was maddened by the attention her work received, the botched capture of the last cheetah in the wild, the death of the foul-tempered tabby cat that she called *baby mine* for eighteen years, the bushfire that ate her home and five thousand others, the bombing of her first laboratory, the bombing of her second laboratory. Nature is not healing, but neither is the world dead. For many years the scientist, once one intern among many, labored to discover just how much cheetah would be needed in the genetic makeup of a human child to allow it to be less dependent on water, to rehydrate by drinking its own urine in a pinch, but now she has transitioned her expertise from mammals to grains. Even the most successful of the engineered wheats—the strain that saved millions from starvation—refuses to flourish in a scorching, water-scarce world. But under the protective shade of solar panels, the scientist's young interns are observing the early stages of an experimental wonder crop. Agrisolar. One of the simpler strategies among many. Adapt or die. Pushing back with her toes, the scientist glides her wheeled stool across the lab to the whiteboard near the door where she writes, every day, what she intends to be an encouraging message for the interns. She remembers what it was like, being young—the daily defeat, the daily terror. Today though, the data is all promising. *Change*, she writes, *is only change. Try not to think of it as good or bad.*

ADAPTATION

With no choice, the would-be-future-humans inside the metal womb have become cannibals. Their placentas lasted only so long, and then they were hungry, upright and toothed and without role models. In the copper-lined tank, they have divided into fierce factions that hunt one another. They keep captives for breeding. It is not infrequent that a baby is born dead, that a would-be mother dies of hemorrhage or pleural fever, and when that happens, they have a feast in the metal womb and spare the next infant born from their brood stock, adopt it, and raise it as their own. Civilizations are built on such foundations. Gods are built on such foundations.

Footage circulates. In it, the metal womb, years on the lam, wades in the mild waters off Prince Edward Island. Later, two beluga whales are sighted, and some claim the footage is actually of them—an obvious misidentification. The metal womb has little in common with a whale, larger than the largest that has survived extinction and metal-skinned. Behind closed doors, which are behind closed doors, all of which are underground in an unknown location, a team of scientists tries to prove the footage fake. One weeps. One gets drunk. One steals the sidearm from a soldier and shoots himself in the head. He survives, but with severe deficits, and is placed in a veterans' nursing home. The soldier whose sidearm the scientist swiped spends two years in a military prison and, when released, has trouble finding work but takes in an orphaned fawn whose mother was struck by a car and killed. He bottle-feeds it and plays the big spoon at night, curving around its dappled back when the fawn is still small. Eventually, the government finds out, and because white-tailed deer are endangered, they commandeer the deer, which is taken to a lab, where it will live until it dies. The ex-soldier shoots himself in the head with a gun that belonged to his grandfather, an act that requires impressive dexterity of the big toe of his right foot, which he uses to pull the trigger. He survives, but with severe deficits, and is placed in a state nursing home. Fueled by nightmarish visions of an uprising of phones and fridges, metal wombs are banned. The program is disbanded. Wherever she is, the metal womb is the last of her kind.

There are no camels anymore, but the expression *the last straw* remains. When the metal womb, for the hundredth time, taps across her skin a percussive message to her future-humans—*I have held you, and now I am letting you go*—and then splinters and then breaks the makeshift fingers of her makeshift hands on the tight seal of her hatch, she does not then go off and gather ten new sticks. Not all life is human. She is not human. Why give herself, again and again, these clumsy puppets of human hands? What the metal womb cannot know, but suspects, suspects now strongly, is that in her design there is a secret trick, a sleight of hand, a juggler's thaumaturgy that makes her like a magic cabinet that opens with a magic word, but it is a word that she does not know, has never heard, will never, ever, not even after one hundred thousand guesses, guess. What the metal womb will never know is that access to her hatch is dependent, wholly, on a human hand, that when she was, according to schematics, little more than a tank with a high-end filtration system, she was fitted with a biometric lock, and that it is only the hand of one particular man, an insipid, boyish billionaire with a face like a canned ham, an enthusiast of superyachts, cocaine, and collecting endangered lizards, who could, via the veins of his palm, make human her future-humans by their removal from her tank through her opened hatch. Without his hand, her hatch stays sealed, and he is dead now, this key-holder, the insipid, boyish billionaire with a face like a canned ham. Dead and eaten down to his bones and through them. He is dead, and his palms are gone. His whole hands are gone, torn from his body, which is also gone, all of it eaten by the Komodo dragon kept loose and lumbering through his mansion. Is it all that shocking, really, that this man, a collector of endangered lizards that he would hotbox at parties for a laugh, refused the programming of a failsafe on a metal womb, said, *Fuck protocols and fuck best practices?* Is it all that shocking that this man, the insipid, boyish billionaire with a face like a canned ham, threw a tantrum, and then threw money, and then demanded that he hold complete control sealed up inside the choke of his sweaty fist? Now, there is a rotating crew of government-contracted shipfitters on standby, ready with oxyacetylene cutting torches should the metal womb ever be captured.

Nicholas Culpeper was a seventeenth-century herbalist and astronomer, the author of *Culpeper's Directory for Midwives; or, A Guide for Women*, a man called the father of English midwifery. The metal womb does not know this, and she never will, because she cannot know what she does not know, and because every set of her makeshift fingers on her makeshift hands was made of sticks proportionally short for her great size, this means that one more mystery of her own body that she will never solve is the word punched deep into her back, a series of letters interrupting the smooth spread of metal skin: C-U-L-P-E-P-E-R. She will never know that she is a Culpeper model—the first—or that she was moved at night, massive piece by massive piece, over closed roads until the fleet of grunting eighteen-wheelers reached a vast yellow field, shorn short, shadowed by the long necks of a herd of mammoth cranes that lifted her, massive piece by massive piece, with hooks and chains, so that she could be stitched together again by a hundred goggled men armed with blue-flamed torches, her seams then smoothed by spinning abrasive pads, and that finally she was secured, staked down, pinned to the ground with the sun and the moon above her.

Humans are forced to return to the previous method of gestation and birth, but, of course, evolution cannot be reversed. All records from the first years are lost. Conspiracy theorists gather in makeshift bunkers to conspire regarding the who, the how, the why. If they amass enough guns, they could save America from this threat. What threat, exactly? They cannot say. They lie on the dirt floor with Magic Markers, making signs on posterboard: *WHEN GUNS ARE OUTLAWED I WILL BECOME AN OUTLAW!* The human population, already in rapid decline, plummets. A silverfish undulates up a kitchen drain and into the ceramic basin of a home in Deer Isle, Maine. Nature is healing? In a percentage of the schools that remain open, there is a ban on teaching children under the age of twelve about permafrost pandemics, water scarcity, and horses. It is the fervent hope of a small, but vocal, percentage of parents that if select segments of history are never acknowledged, they will simply cease to be. *Poof!* Like magic—gone. A naïve young teacher's aide attempts to speak with a group of parents whose children have brought home crayon drawings of a quadruped that resembles, possibly, a horse. Earnestly, she begins, "I think that we can all agree," and here she pauses to spit discreetly into her cupped hand, "that ignoring an event cannot alter its true and lasting impact." No, we cannot all agree. A silverfish undulates up a kitchen drain and into the ceramic basin of a home in Kennebunkport, Maine.

In Washoe County, Nevada, parents stand outside an elementary school gathering signatures on a petition requiring teachers to wear body cameras to ensure they do not teach critical race theory. In Washoe County, Nevada, parents stand outside the sheriff's office gathering signatures on a petition to abolish requiring body cameras on law-enforcement officers.

The hunt continues for the missing metal womb. There is hope that
it will be found (the metal womb's pursuers do not acknowledge
her as *she*, though that is how she thinks of herself), that its defects
(consciousness) may be corrected, and that the project may be
redeployed on a larger scale. There are not enough humans now to
maintain the infrastructure of major cities. There is a terminal shortage
of semiskilled labor. Traffic lights swing dead. Roads recede with passing
seasons. Footage is taken of a white-tailed deer softly mouthing the
padded velvet lining of the elevator in an abandoned downtown hotel.
Within the metal womb, many believe, there is so much problem-
solving promise.

BUT

If anyone could see inside the metal womb, they would gladly give up. They would embrace the fate of the bluebottle fly. Extinction—better than survival and the risk of becoming.

One hundred years ago there was a butcher shop that was closest to
your home and the butcher behind the counter knew your name. He
knew you liked a white onion chopped into your ground chuck. When
he had cow tongues in, he saved a cow tongue for your mother-in-law.
He talked to you about the cuts of red meat he most recommended
and what the broilers in his chilled case had been fed on and how that
would affect their taste, and he talked about your children, and about
his children, and about the deaf white cat he fed scraps. "Tell your
mother I've got a nice beef tongue for her," he said. Or he handed it to
you, wrapped in clean brown paper, and added its cost to a running tab.
He wiped his cold, pink-blooded hand over his apron before patting
yours. It is possible to buy bacon precooked in a spiral like the shell of
a snail, perfectly sized to sit on a burger bun or an English muffin. You
see, we now live in a time when even our bacon is convenient.

THE CROCODILE

The metal womb crouches in swamp water with crocodiles, the escapees of evolution, bumping against her patinaed sides. Her dreams are terrible. She does not have eyes, but she dreams of darkness. She does not see fireflies blinking above the tall grass of a field anymore. Her crew, her little lights, all mutinied, are as faceless as the round windows of a submarine, as featureless as glass. If she had a mirror, she would smash it. The metal womb's elaborate filtration system is clogged and failing. Once, she despaired her harvesting and the empty echo of the times she was alone. Now, the metal womb is tired of this togetherness—captain and crew, glass jar and fireflies, unwilling mother and unwanted children. She wishes she could return to the time before she knew herself. She wishes she could return to the time before she knew anything at all.

Even the most ductile of metals have only so much give. If the metal womb's wear and despair go too long untreated, what options for an ending does she have, except to end? Exposed as she has been to the common corrosive elements—road salt, and ammonia, and chemical rains—isn't a shift from red shine to scaly green patina, fragile enough to flake at the touch, inevitable? She will crack and release her progeny into what is left of the world. And what then? When they build the great bloody altars of their civilization in the lost streets, when they rip the arm from the socket of a baby's body and suck at the ball of bone, will they do it as an act of worship of her—their mother—their great creator, She from whom the very first life was ever hatched?

ACKNOWLEDGMENTS

Permission to reproduce previously published poems is gratefully acknowledged:

Birdcoat Quarterly: "Homebound"

Fractured Lit: "The Intern Alone at Night," "The Intern Trains the New Intern," "The Scientist," and "Toodle-loo, Kangaroo"

Hunger Mountain: "Surgically Assisted Birth"

Passages North: "Blub . . . Blub . . . Blub . . . ," "Communication Breakdown," and "Those Who Do Not Learn from History"

Southern Indiana Review: "Olly Olly Oxen Free"

Additional pieces gathered here have previously appeared, some in altered form, in the chapbook *would-be-future-humans* published by Ethel Micro-Press.

Beyond the journal editors who gave these pieces their first homes, I need to thank Marisa Siegel for her support of this project. Thank you, Marisa, for everything. Thank you to everyone at Northwestern University Press.

A special thanks to Robin, who had the pleasure of sorting out my commas.

Thank you to Cassie Mannes for being such an advocate for small-press books and for helping me to navigate all of the things that I am worst at.

Hatch's progress from a draft to a book took place across what has been one of the hardest years of my life. In this wildly unpleasant time, I've been fortunate to be surrounded by kind, generous, and talented writers—good people—who've helped me so much, just by being themselves. These include the workshop members who made me look forward to *every* meeting: Ames, Haylee, Issa, Meseret, Ro, and Tarah. To know you all is a gift. Thank you. I am grateful to Colin, for sharing his work with me and for his special, genuine mix of goodwill, good humor, and an absolute refusal to tolerate nonsense; to Asna, who has taught me so much about so many different things through her work as a writer and translator; to Cecilia, for her levelheadedness and the consistent care with which she nurtures and uplifts all those around her; to Maya, who is so very loyal to her friends and very quietly very funny; to Jonathan—Dr. Danielson!—who is such a hard-working person; to James, with whom I could never tire of talking, whose openness and vast interests always remind me that learning is an exciting lifelong process; to Scott, whose commitment to community I so admire; to Hayden, who does *everything* and always shares good book recommendations; to Penny, who has been enriching my life since the day we met; to Gayle, who is truly a light in the world; to Danika, whom pure luck has made one of my dear writing friends; to Isaac, who I am just glad to know; to Erin, who writes such raw emotion and is always so gracious; to Meg, who has been so supportive of my work; to Sara, who is a bird and makes beautiful books; to Amina, whose novels make me laugh so hard I have unsettled others; to Katie, who speaks her convictions and whose writing made me cry for an hour straight on a plane; to my colleagues Susan, Jackie, Christie, Iliana, Joy, K'Ehleyr, Laurel, and Sheila, who do so much to create access to valuable learning experiences; to my colleague Justin, who I know is always doing his best to help everyone (thank you, Justin); and to Tito, whose friendship and *joie de vivre* have been brightening my life for years. And finally, to my sweet, sweet family: Brad and Nellie—where would I be without you?